LAYING WAYS

Scripta Humanistica

Directed by
BRUNO M. DAMIANI
The Catholic University of America

ADVISORY BOARD

Mechthild Cranston

LAYING WAYS

TEXTS AND PRE-TEXTS

With a Foreword by Germaine Brée

$\mathfrak{Scripta\ Humanistica}$

71

1990

Library of Congress Cataloging-in-Publication Data
  Cranston, Mechthild.
    Laying ways : texts and pre-texts / Mechthild Cranston ; with a
  foreword by Germaine Brée.
    p.   cm. -- (Scripta Humanistica ; 71)
    ISBN 978-0-916379-77-3 : $26.50
    I. Title. II. Series: Scripta Humanistica (Series) ; 71.
  PS3553.R2736L3   1990
  811'.54--dc20   90-38828
                                             CIP

                    Publisher and Distributor:
                    SCRIPTA HUMANISTICA
                       1383 Kersey Lane
                  Potomac, Maryland 20854 U.S.A.

                    SCRIPTA HUMANISTICA

For G./C.

Quanti dolci pensier, quanto disio . . .

CONTENTS

II. DANCES

III. AND DUST

FOREWORD

"In the uneven/ Dark bricks/ We had edged/ Fresh paths to surface/ From the charred foundations/ Underneath the crabgrass/ . . . ." The opening lines of "Laying Ways," the poem which lent its title to the present collection, concentrate in a single image the poetic process, creative and healing. Mechthild Cranston was born in Berlin. Poem by poem those "fresh paths" leading out of a dark past of fear and loss emerge, reaching out to perceptions of light, beauty, love, and the sense of a shared humanity. "Hostias et Preces," the title of another poem, suggests the rites of exorcism, "charms," incantations implicit in the web of the writing. The three parts indicated ("Ways," "Dances," "And Dust") can be read as three somewhat muted modulations of that process, a musical structure that gives the volume a moving unity: the will to celebrate rather than to give way to the "imprecations" suffering can inspire.

A brief "Pre-Text" presents an account of how the young scholar--well-known in academia for her numerous professional activities: her energetic participation in many a colloquium, her critical oeuvre (books, articles, edited journals and reviews), her familiarity with the arcane language and procedures of the more complex systems of critical theory, her easy access to literature in five languages--came to discover the way to the "creative discourse" that shapes these poems. Surprisingly it was an NEH summer seminar on the state of contemporary criticism that was the agent of that discovery. Surprisingly, until one learns that Geoffrey Hartman,

1

of Yale, was the director of the seminar, a poet-scholar himself to whom
with characteristic generosity Mechthild Cranston expresses her gratitude.

It has perhaps been one of the weaknesses of literary criticism to ap-
proach texts from some holistic point of view, explicating, then decon-
structing the explicatory patterns, leaving aside the basic impact of the
texts themselves on the imagination, the sensibility and awareness of
readers. What Geoffrey Hartman brought to his fellow-readers, it seems,
was a sense of the poetic function of the creative process of writing be-
yond but through its technical exigencies. Criticism and creation have
often been considered an antagonistic pair. And yet who would deny
that, as readers, creators have often been the more illuminating critics,
whatever their theoretical stance. Mechthild Cranston, in any case, had
started to write poems and essays before the empowering experience of
the seminar. She had lived, from the beginning, in an aura of heightened
awareness that her friends, like myself, have always sensed. The seminar,
as it were, "way-laid" her to reveal the interplay of language, critical
lucidity and technical mastery in the act of reading deep layers of memory
that illuminate and integrate the scattered, fragmentary, quotidian pres-
ence of a lived reality, outer and inner, at one and the same time held in
the space of a poem.

A familiar imagery--free of conscious symbolism--is woven into the fabric
of these texts: beaches, shells, ships, tides keenly observed; the play of
light as day passes into night, or from night to day; as winter moves to-

2

ward spring and spring to summer and autumn. Places like Key West, or Proust's fictional Combray, appear side by side: motifs, among others, in a tapestry peopled with human figures encountered along the way of the "we," the elusive lovers who, wiser than Dante's Paolo and Francesca, will read "on and on." Love is at the center of the poet's itinerary. One feels the presence of a keen and unflinching "eye" within the text, and withal an "I" gentle and compassionate in a deeply humane way.

Laying Ways is an appealing and "charming" book with which it is, I feel, an honor and a pleasure to be associated.

Germaine Brée

PRE-TEXT

More than ten years ago now, thirteen young NEH scholars from
throughout the United States descended for the summer into a breathless
Yale basement to hear an eminent master ponder the state of contempo-
rary criticism.

It was not long, however, before most of us realized that what we were
asked to share in fact was not a critical state ruled by a master, but a
creative process which at its best came very close to the collective birthing
of original texts.

When the summer ended, Geoffrey Hartman made to all of us the gift
of a sonnet, and entrusted to one of the participants--who ran a
handletter press--his collection of poetry which came to be published as
Akiba's Children.

From our musings that summer on the interplay of creative and critical
discourse emerged other poems, some of the present texts and pre-texts
among them.

Laying Ways is thus dedicated to "my cat Geoffrey," but also to others
along the road who have seen and seized the possibilities of
critical/creative thought: Germaine Brée (without whom, for me, the

Yale summer would not have been) and Harold Bloom, as well as those unnamed.

It has become commonplace to say that texts beget other texts, an assumption that is, in part, true. In the present collection, for example, "Breton Hymn" began as a take-off on Breton's *"L'Union libre."* The poem *"Kristallnacht"* followed upon the reading of Marguerite Duras' *Les Yeux bleus cheveux noirs.* But it also followed the public event of the Holocaust, the private experience of the Berlin Blockade, and the shared tensions of a midnight bus ride from New York to Philadelphia.

The poems collected here, laying ways for (and waylaying) the telling of besieged cities and open seas have been illuminated in part by artists who in other media opened our eyes to the seeing of things: Paul Klee and Henry Moore foremost among them. Again, though, *"Angelus dubiosus"* owes more to the presence of Geoffrey Hartman than to the painting of Paul Klee.

Running counter to the modern mode of striking images, the texts of *Laying Ways* have, ultimately, very few visual pre-texts. Their lines flow, more frequently, from half-remembered sounds: flute and bassoon concerti, notes of a requiem sung as a child and heard again in an Italian film, Spoleto festival overtures, the swish of summer islands and autumn walks.

6

Lands laid waste, at times, by the impossibility of telling, and saved, at others, by ways found through the text. Poems that, like Paolo and Francesca, so often began and ended with two hands touching upon a page: pre-ludes and pre-texts to the unfinished business of living.

All, nonetheless, songs of praise and thanksgiving for those--named and unnamed--present at the birthing.

Mechthild Cranston
Summer 1990

I. WAYS

ANCIENT VESSELS

The beach at dawn was clear of footsteps
Shells lay
Open but intact
In rhythmic patterns

At our heels
The rasping sands
Called back the women
Come
All summer long across the dunes

Ancient vessels
Spilling with the tides
Against the moon

Rising now
In full view

Of the lighthouse.

EDEN PLACE

The door was opened and the morning
Air stood clear up on the hill
Whiffs of falling flowers borne
In passing clouds there was the chill

Of autumn settling on the branches
Dust of leaves sheets folded back
Breath withheld vague fingers reaching
Holy unremembered texts

They rose Naked by the door
Light stood mid day
And nothing now was as before

The feast where no word was where they
In knowledge bore the tree and cast
The golden fruit to mortal beast.

BLUEFISH AT BRISTOL

Flies screened in past midnight the full moon
Turned up the brown-backed players the guitars
So useless in this place so out of tune
With the receding tides there were no cars

Past nine and bluefish grilled on private beaches
Signaled the close of day We came upon
Our separate rooms in total darkness each his
Own keeper of the stair each clothed in his own

Skin From down below the ship-rocked bay
Sent up at noon a fresh supply of singers
And the softer call of gulls The day
We knew would be no stranger if the swimmers
Racing toward the unremembered coast
Waved to us

Naked as they passed.

PRISM

The summer was late
We stood in the rain
Watching the spectra
Our bodies made
Claiming the rainbow
Naked
At our feet

Two faces
Meeting
At the edge
Of the prism.

VOICES

The way to bed
Is lit by fireflies
Crickets crank up
For the night

We count down
By the absent voice

Owls
Greet the dawn.

KEY WEST

Summer without end . . .

The old women here
All hang their tangled
Hair
From trees

Tiny blue
Bells float
On air

Men suck
Cold shrimp
Steamed
In beer

Children
On the coral reef
Chase the heron

Sponges
Are sold in pairs

And all
Is as before
Here

All here
As before

Order and Time
However clear.

17

COMBRAY

for Germaine Brée

I have stayed too long
In the shuttered space
Of sleep what ecstasy
May come what dreams

Give me the mornings
Of expanding breath
Shifting steeples
And uneven streets

Lights that break
In untold
Flame

Seeds that scattering
Unfold
Come to speak their name.

EVENT

Lie still

The wind with gentle fingers will
Push back your hair
And softly brush
Against your skin

The bird is hushed
The sun stands tall

And from the valley
Burning forests
Signal
The event

Listen

The leaf itself has stirred
The shadows lifted
And your body
Opened
To the call.

VOLO UT SIS

You raise the overflowing cup
Gently to your lips
Press down

The night is far
And still
You come

To take and fill
The soft dark chalice
With your praise.

LAYING WAYS

In the uneven
Dark bricks
We had edged
Fresh paths to surface
From the charred foundations
Underneath the crabgrass

We had inched into the clay
To the audible confusion and displeasure
Of stray cats
Unscented slabs of stone to mark
The just raked center of the earth

Here at noon
The guests appeared
To break the bread together
Toast the weather with new Beaujolais
And speak of France

Learned responses
Bounced off starched tablecloths

Transparent clockwork
Behind double glass

Hands limited to touch
Of salt and wine
Passing

Toward evening
As rough pine bark shavings
By the truckload spread
In geometric patterns at our feet
The healthful smell of European baths

They that had stayed too long
Fearing a lack of clothes and muddy boots and colds
Leave as if
Drawn
By the cleaner definitions
Of the walk

Into the charmed foundation
Of a new moon

Going toward May.

II. DANCES

BRETON HYMN

My woman of algae
And amber eyes
My woman of ice
And of taffy thighs
My woman of vice

Of spindrift
Hair
My woman of lies
And air

My woman of whale
And of speckled stone
My woman of tarred and jaundiced bone
My woman of sighs and
My woman alone

My woman of summer
And winter green
My woman of spleen
And ideal my
Woman of seaweed and dream

My woman with breasts of foam
Of Star
And jelly
Fish belly
Of tongue
And nostril
Of spray my woman
Of Jonas and Moby
Of yes
And maybe
My woman of No

My woman of beacon and beckon
Of beach and pebble
My woman the rebel
Of sperm and roe

My woman of spume
And stern my woman
Of shell and must

Of lust
And hell

Of blood and water
And mud
My woman of rust
Of birth

And forgetting
And curse
My woman
Of always and ever and

Now

My woman
Of earth.

BASSOON & CAT

Huge brown yellow-rimmed
It loomed between long legs
To sit
Air-tight
Suspension
Of the lips

The sebaceous
Hairless head
Now and then
Leaned right to spit
On the dense
ly lit
Hot stage

And silvery fingers sensuous
ly slid
Down the polished tube to make
Music
Of all this

The black cat
Furry beyond compare
And turning
Right to left

Opts
For the unheard melodies

And drier weather.

OYSTER & WORLD

I hear the oyster
In my plate
Masturbate masturbate

Masturbate
Until too late
Happy healthy muscular
Voraciously
She's ate
(Vaguely virginal
To taste)

I see the necklace
In the glass
See and am
That fruit of sand
And sickness born
To make the oyster
Last

The parasitic worm
The irritation
From within
The avarice
That dares

Disturb
The world's
Hermetic pearl

The hard core
Masturbation

With a grin.

BLOOM

for Harold Bloom

The women in the room
Grow hot at noon
He wants a sweater
No one's got

I am older than you my dears and colder
I have children
More tired than you
Says Bloom's

Baritone
Shaking at will
Till
Bloom's boy's turtle
Adjusting his neck
To the sun
Like Christopher's frog
Creeps into the room

34

But he's in the Lake Country
Sleeping with God

Knows whom the women grow hotter
A sensory assault
Bloom cut his hair
He is cold

Bishop and Stevens are
Drawn to each other
By mother

The world is presence not form
Bloom holds the watch of his father

If muses are mothers
Of memory and memory
The only form of cognition
Pray love remember
The father
And mother's
Perdition

The high noon
Purple extends
The juxtaposition of text
And sense never he says

Quite innocent

The women burn
Words
Without sweater
Bloom (aesthetically moved)
Speaks of unforgiving the text
And the letter

The more time passes the later it gets
They chuckle

Bloom buckles up
The women sit tall

Well my dears
Good luck to us all
He shuffles

Children of Bloom
Down the hall's
Golden parentheses
Flower and
Head for the pool.

CALHOUN CORNERS AT FIVE

He had chosen this place
She thought
For reasons of space
Backing
Against the wall

He
Asking to move
His chair
Closer to her
Makes her laugh

Till

Crippled by refraction
Clashing glasses catch
The quiet
Where they sit
Heads
Steady now

While bodies
Waiting to be drunk
Like hard pressed vine
Choose not to run

Cauterized in time
And wary

Of the sunset.

TOE TOUCH

Toes tangled
In the ropes
Reach for the trees
Turning
The afternoon
To profit

The unordinary
Bird
Retreats
Leaving the heavy hour
After five
To its own undoing
Of the clouds

There is no netting
Fire or rain.

COLOR OF LEAVES

The season's first pine
Sent up the neighbor's chimney
Has a clean
Pungent smell

Bees
Swarming like they'd never see
The sun again
Make their last honey
Of Coppertone
And smoke

Bare
Backed
Against the house
The women stand

Quiet faces in
The long last
Sun-sucked afternoon

Taut pillars of brick and skin
Beaten
By the high-pitched winds

Like ancient drums
The color of leaves.

GLASPERLENSPIEL

Glass beads hung from the branches
Chance meeting upon the land
Naked we
Like the seasons
Walk softly
Behind the trees

Linking hands.

WITCH DANCE

She rides the flames of autumn
As her hands
Fold in the untold
Secrets
Of the land

And from the mountain
Winds descend
To frame her burning body
And the branch

Bared swiftly
To the circling cloud
Commands

The hallowed ground
To ripen
Toward the dance.

MOORE

He lifts his hand against the sky
Measuring the risks
Slow rotations of the wrist
Take full measure of the light
In descending half-steps

He is pleased:

Here past noon the stone may come to stand
Here the body clasped
By its own hands resolve
To dance

Here the shadows
Cast by shiftless eyes
Raise up visions of time steadied
In delivered space.

HOSTIAS ET PRECES

You came upon us like a falling
Star in August summer dark and
Deep into the night of drunken
Glass Fields broken with the

Drought and cattle near the harvest
Died We walked the foothills and the
Garden delicate with fruit and
Blossoms of relentless

White And still there was a song
About us like the flight of birds
At our rising fall rains

Spoke a blessing not much
Else There was a healing on
The waters tall winds came and danced.

III. AND DUST

BLACK BUTTERFLY

The golden grain
Displayed by open palms
The double arch
Stretched from the grass to cloud

The fingering
That breaks the ground
Where the ripe fruit
May grow and fall

Call in the quiet
Space of dusk
The fourfold name

The passing touch
Of dark wings:

Dust to dust.

CHERRIES

And take from seventy springs . .

Looking into his own eyes he saw
Seventy springs
Beyond sickness

Changing women
Deliver the water
And children

Hands cupped
Come to the secret still

Dark place of the cherries.

FEAST OF INGATHERING

Seven candles
An armful of flowers
A room at the desert inn
Of the bird
The dry pool

What more
At the end of that leaning
Road
Shall I remember that
Swallowed the sun

There was the failure
Of course
And the smell
Of hair
Burning
The stairs
Wind
Leading nowhere

And then

Call it fear or forgetting
Or curse
The seering vision
That I had been
Miles before you and memories longer
To the desert
Inn of the bird

If the flowers still hold
And the pool fills again
Will we then
Remember
The feast and the children
Faster than fire
Driving the road that buries the sun

Shall they be told then
There was
No room at the inn?

RHIZOMES

The unmitigated clumps of iris
Hugging their last inch of surface soil
(And each other)
Have spread further
Down and deeper
Like some archaic
Humped thing
To the air-tight
Underground of hardened mud

Spring rains have struck
No fire from the green
No goddess came
Nor birth
To pry
The ancient flower
From the sword

No one to speak
The word's renewed

Detachment
From the root

No one to lift the veil
No one to break
The earth that shields

The still dark unison
Toward death.

OUTING

The smell was
Of honey and gas
And wet wind
Over the mountain grass

He claimed not to know
The color of mushrooms

It didn't
Last.

RUTH

Blue
Was her favorite
Color
And there was
But one way to do
Bacon
Dishes
Beds

The world was wholesome
Tidy clean
Tiny
Blue-ribboned
Boxes
With tissue
Paper in between

You washed your hands
At her house and brushed teeth
Three times a day
Drank Listerine

Pinned back your hair
Induced
Irregularity
And dream
Much here was show
And some things real

Flowers
Sweet peas
Pyracantha
Ripe with berries
White in spring

Fruit she brought
From out the desert
Biggest any
One had seen

And roses
Always roses

Her love of trees
And the ability
To marvel

Over again
And over
At the green
On her trips East

Sons not coming
Home for Christmas
Daughters
On the run
Memory
Of Wellesley
Waltzes
Rolling
In the fields

She returns now
To the shadows
And the shade
Of ancient hills

Where the smell
Of lilac lingers
And the tall blue willows
Dance.

HEADING SOUTH

Into the once white quilt
Stained by the curse now
And discarded
You will rake

Poplar ash and oak
Tree memories you hold
The way they cradle children
Wind the shroud
Around your mother
Way out
West

You don't go
To the edge
To check on summer
Serpents or on snakes
Being
Of no consequence
To autumn

A girl in yellow
Stops to ask
The way the circle winds
You know
Though you don't live here
Now

Above
The first November
Mountains
Moons
Like pumpkins
Spot the night

We shall have rain
Tomorrow
And much wind

More leaves to rake
And the dark
Woman
Heading South.

CAT & SPOON

A time before
Whatever shepherds watched
Lay still moons jumped the night
The travelers stopped

Up on the hill the wind
And stained glass angels
Fracturing the light
Rose up We woke

I brushed
A snowflake
From your dream

The fragile
Space of death
The shutters snapped.

ANGELUS DUBIOSUS

for Paul Klee

We touched upon the Prelude
Like Paolo preying on a book
Omphalic intimations of the text
To build on hell the intercourse of sense

The wind was very gentle and yet urgent
To plant a voice among the vine

That day we did read on and on
The wings of the averted angel
Named and caught
And laid to rest
In language and in time
The dark child:

Terrified.

KRISTALLNACHT

He held her
To the prism his delight
In crystal breaking
With the candled room

Against the daylight
Made their hands
Fall where the sword had
Brushed against the fire

Brief like a window
Shattering
Their eyes meet   Cry

As others would make love
In the scattering of stars:
The open prison.

NOT THE WORD ONLY

Your hand upon the page
Inflamed
Not the word
Only

Fire is
Absence of touch

Lest there be
Another burning

Of books and no
One left to plant

The raw material
Of ashes.

DUSK TO DAWN

They shared the forest and
The golf green lawn ran
Past the terrace where at dusk
Mocking birds spread out
Their mating call

They propped up pillows poured
The wine and settled
Into song At midnight
No one saw
The empty glass
And lips that ran
A prayer past the unknown gods

Where no one slept
The air was still and
Dawn came hard
To separate beds

Spread for the breaking
Of the bread

And empty

Nests.

PAGE PROOF

I run my hand across the page
Proof mutable
As skin

And feel the syllables rescind
The humid summer
That was you

Bent bodies
Pressed
Into suspense

Burnt offerings
Far less innocent
Than ink
Dried into print.

Acknowledgments

Some of the poems in this collection have appeared in small magazines, arts journals, and poetry anthologies, as listed below:

"Color of Leaves," "Ancient Vessels," "Laying Ways," "Hostias et Preces," and "Bluefish at Bristol" in *The Arts Journal.*

"Bluefish at Bristol," "Combray," "Angelus dubiosus," and "Dusk to Dawn" in *American Poetry Anthology.*

"Event" in *Mosaic;* "Cherries" in *The Locust Post,* and "Heading South" in *The Wayah Review.*

Acknowledgment is made to the editors for permission to reprint.

Scripta Humanistica

Directed by
BRUNO M. DAMIANI
The Catholic University of America
COMPREHENSIVE LIST OF PUBLICATIONS *

BOOK ORDERS

* Clothbound. *All book orders,* except library orders, must be prepaid and addressed to **Scripta Humanistica**, 1383 Kersey Lane, Potomac, Maryland 20854. *Manuscripts* to be considered for publication should be sent to the same address.